ginger
the flavours & the flowers

petra frieser

Dedicated to nature

        ... because nature just *is*.

Ginger - the flavours and the flowers
By Petra Frieser

Designed by Pebbles in the Sky
Photography by Petra Frieser

Published by Pebbles in the Sky 2006

Pebbles in the Sky
PO Box 1975
Sunshine Plaza, QLD 4558
www.pebblesinthesky.com.au

© 2006 Text Petra Frieser
© 2006 Images Petra Frieser

Printed in Australia by Fergies Print & Mail, Brisbane, Australia

The National Library of Australia Cataloguing-in-Publication Data:
Frieser, Petra
 Ginger : the flavours and the flowers.

Includes Bibliography and Index
ISBN 9780980306804

1.Ginger. 2. Cookery (Ginger). I. Title

633.83

ginger

the flavours & the flowers

petra frieser

pebbles in the sky

contents

the introduction

Ginger is many things to many people. Most of us know ginger as a flavour, a spicy addition to cakes and breads, the zing in an Asian dish or the fresh burst in a salad. Others will know ginger as the hedonistic aroma of burning incense or base note of an exotic perfume or then, perhaps, they will know it as a colour, an earthy tone vibrant and full of energy.

It is more than likely that the first introduction to one of the various varieties of ginger is how ginger will continue to be perceived and reactions can be as varied as its kaleidoscope of flowers and flavours. My first ginger experience was glacé ginger and not a good one at that. As an eight year old the shock surprise of choosing the choc-coated glacé ginger out of what was surely a delectable box of chocolates otherwise, resulted in a 15-year-long abhorrence at so much as the word! Then one day my son brought home two bags brimming with ginger rhizomes, the bounty of a school excursion to The Ginger Factory, at Yandina, Queensland and a neighbouring farm. Knowing that I loved to cook, he no doubt thought that he had brought home the ultimate prize... Not wanting to disappoint, I set about trying to find ways in which to utilise this exasperating amount of ginger. I am not quite sure what actually happened to it all, but I do know that it was a major turning point in my relationship with ginger.

It was after this that I began to discover ginger plants, dozens of different varieties, not necessarily all true gingers but in the genre that is commonly referred to as gingers. My first favourite was cardamom (dwarf cardamom in this instance) a ginger relation. This cardamom plant won my heart by its predisposition to being almost unkillable by my, although willing, yet somewhat incapable green thumbs and the delicious fragrance that the foliage released when bruised or brushed against sealed it. What was even better was its ability to multiply, or more accurately, to be divided, as is the

7

case with most ginger species, allowing me to fill spaces in the garden everywhere with its beautiful lush foliage. I wasn't actually aware of their flowers at first until one year I was pleasantly surprised by pendulous clusters of orchid-like blossoms.

My fascination with ginger flowers grew gradually, more out of preference for the plant's hardiness on a block of land that had more obstacles than I could conquer. Their realm of beautiful flowers was an unexpected bonus but a welcome one and there the passion began. So, it would seem I have an undeniable penchant for the extravagant floral displays that are attributed to the ginger family. Ginger flowers will literally stop me in my tracks in the garden as I am filled with awe and amazement. Their intricacy is astounding, their beauty overwhelming and, in some instances, their fragrance absolutely intoxicating. They are a visual pleasure and one that I can't imagine ever tiring of.

On the following pages I will share my passion and explore some of these exquisite flowers alongside the myriad wonderful flavours derived from this gnarled family of rhizomes that has induced ginger in its various states to be such a large part of my life. I hope that others can also appreciate the extraordinary beauty of these flowers alongside the versatility of its flavour. As for glacé ginger, well, I have rediscovered it as well – I really don't know what all the fuss was about! Enjoy!

the history

Ginger has a rich and well-travelled history. Although no one is exactly sure where it originates from, ginger has managed to weave itself into the cultural fabric of many lands making it among the most sought-after spices in the world. Ginger stems from the Sanskrit word 'sringa-vera' meaning 'horn body' or 'antler shaped', which is understandable considering its antler-like appearance although rather unromantic for a spice so interlaced with heated suggestion and having such an evocative reputation. India recognises a spiritual connection to ginger and attributes it to 'awakening one's inner fire of divinity and creativity', which I rather like the idea of. It is also thought to be a fragrance of valour and courage and deemed by many as an aphrodisiac resulting in its soaring popularity through many periods of time.

Ginger travelled well and this hardy rhizome saw itself transported from China and India to fertile growing regions all over the world; the West Indies, Jamaica, the Mediterranean, Europe, Africa and eventually to Australia where in Queensland it has become a major industry. It was China that initially preserved ginger as early as the 16th Century, though since then our own Buderim Ginger has come to account for a large percentage of the world's processed ginger in its various states.

The Buderim Ginger story is itself unique. Some raw ginger roots having found their way to Buderim on the Sunshine Coast, became the foundation for the Buderim Ginger Growers Cooperative formed by five Buderim farmers in an old blacksmiths shop in 1941. It was an endeavour that was to provide an opportunity for growers to expand their sales that became so successful it saw the relocation of their small Buderim facility to a much larger premises in Yandina in 1980, where the success story has continued ever since.

Buderim Ginger is now recognised as a global leader in confectionery ginger with an ever-expanding product range – pickled gingers, crystallised ginger, candied ginger, ginger syrups, marmalades and jams, confectionery - many of which are utilised in the recipes that follow.

The Buderim Ginger site is also the home of The Ginger Factory, which boasts something special in itself. Over the years it has earned the reputation as being a popular tourist attraction for thousands of Sunshine Coast visitors, it is also a venue with one of the most spectacular ginger gardens I have ever seen. If you are fortunate enough to travel to the Sunshine Coast during the summer months, the gardens are a must-see and an awe-inspiring tribute to the ginger flower and all its relating species.

As a flower, ginger has a rich history of its own. Plant collectors of the 1800's prospered though scouring the lush tropical forests of Asia to bring back to Europe spectacular ginger specimens that would become the prize of glasshouses throughout the Victorian era. Soaring heating costs eventually saw the demise of these glasshouses, though the flowers have survived as prizes to more suited climates in which they are now grown for a prosperous cut flower industry. It is here that Queensland is fortunate. Having an ideal climate, many gingers grow easily in even the most tangled of gardens. The result is a huge expansion in its already voluminous number of species alongside the development of some truly breathtaking hybrids, which leads me quite easily to conclude that ginger's history may only be beginning.

the flavour

Ginger, as far as the flavour goes, is the chameleon of the spice world. Ginger flavours are quite varied owing to the numerous methods in which the rhizomes can be preserved. Raw fresh ginger roots have a hot, almost peppery flavour that it is neither savoury nor sweet, allowing a great degree of versatility in its use.

Ginger can be pickled and dried or crystallised, a form in which it has come to be a popular confection known also as candied ginger or glacé ginger. Crystallised ginger is used largely in sweets and chocolates or eaten plain as a sweet by itself, soaked in syrup or sugar coated. Ginger in its other states is served fresh or pickled in salads and dressings, dried in cakes and cookies, ground into pastes or preserved in lemon juice, as well as being adapted into a multitude of conserves and syrups, both savoury and sweet.

In the family of edible gingers there is also galangal and turmeric. They are similar to ginger in their appearance though much earthier in flavour. Turmeric is the more vivid of the two, having a bright orange flesh. Both are generally used either fresh or dried and are a common ingredient in curry pastes as well as other Asian dishes, imparting their own unique, often quite piquant flavours to the dishes to which they are added. A less common edible ginger is the flower of the *Etlingera elatior.* Its spectacular towering torch-like flowers, almost too beautiful to eat, are used in Asian cookery where the flowerheads are usually eaten fresh in salads. Last, but certainly not least, are the aromatic leaves of species such as the Alpinia. Yet another application of the ginger plant in Asian cookery, more often than not the leaves are used to wrap up exotic edible morsels and the leaves are also added to various dishes.

So you see, in the ginger world there is plenty of room left for experimentation, combinations still to be discovered and the lesser-known flavours yet to be explored.

the $ flower

There are so many different species of ginger flowers and within these species many sub species. The *Zingiberaceae* family encompasses most of these ginger species, however there are a few gingers that are not within this family and although they are not considered true gingers they are still often referred to as gingers, defined by their vigorous rhizomes rather than their correct botanical names. The flowers, as they are nearly always referred to, are in fact the inflorescence or bracts, a flowerhead for a multitude of minuscule to mammoth 'actual' flowers, some quite spectacular, which emerge from their protective cloaks individually or in spasmodic clusters, fading and withering as others freshly unfold. The *Zingibers* are the most common ginger. The culinary ginger amongst them, the flowers bracts are generally beehive in shape in a number of attractive colour variations making them a popular cut flower. *Heliconias* could possibly be the most popular of the ginger flowers. In a family of their own, these hardy plants produce endless floral displays, owing to them becoming synonymous with Queensland gardens and tropical gardening. Then there are the *Costus*, beautiful spiralling beauties with orchid like flowers that are sweetly scented and *Curcumas*, hidden surprises in the depth of their own luscious foliage. They are all beautiful.

Ginger plants are not difficult to grow. Most species prefer sheltered positions, but providing they have plenty of organic matter will often do quite well in sunnier positions. Generally, the rhizomes don't need watering during winter - too much moisture will cause the rhizomes to rot.

When you discover ginger flowers, it is hard to pick a favourite. Each is unique and each is individually structured in only a way that nature can achieve; luxurious textures, complex patterns, vibrant colours and heavenly scents. I have often sat for many moments looking into these works of art, admiring their awe-inspiring intricacy, always coming to the same conclusion – how freakish nature really is.

Ginger Pesto

Ginger Pesto is one of the most fabulous things that you can make with fresh ginger. The mint really offsets the ginger. I prefer to pound the ingredients rather than process them, as it gives the pesto a much nicer texture.

Ingredients:

1 bunch mint (approx 1 cup)

1 bunch coriander (approx 1 cup)

2 cloves garlic

25g macadamia nuts

2 tbs fresh ginger

½ cup olive oil

Salt to taste

Method:

Place all the ingredients into a mortar and pound with a pestle (or place in a food processor).

Serve with fresh, crusty bread or as a condiment to accompany meat, fish and vegetable dishes.

the zingiber

Common Varieties:

Zingiber nivium – Milky Way Ginger; *Zingiber officinale* – Common Culinary Ginger; *Zingiber ottensii* – Cocoa Delight Ginger; *Zingiber spectiblis* – Beehive Ginger; *Zingiber zerumbert* – Wild Ginger or Shampoo Ginger.

The Zingiber genus is the most common of all gingers in the *Zingiberaceae* family. There are as many as 150 species, the common edible ginger among them. Although most Zingiber rhizomes are edible, the less common varieties are mostly grown for their amazing torch-like flowers, stems of which shoot directly from the rhizomes. The stems are crowned with a conical inflorescence, its overlapping nectar-filled bracts opening slightly to allow small orchid-like flowers to appear. Easy enough to grow, they tend to prefer sheltered positions.

Falafe with Ginger Minted Yoghurt Sauce

Falafe are perfect as finger food at parties, they have a fresh taste, the ginger giving them that extra zest. The Ginger Minted Yoghurt Sauce adds zest to lamb or when drizzled over steamed vegetables.

Ingredients:

100g dried split broad beans

100g dried chickpeas

1/2 tsp sea salt

11/2 cups fresh coriander, roots removed

1 tbs ground coriander

1 tbs ground cumin

1 tsp grated ginger

1 small red chilli

1/2 onion, finely chopped

1 clove garlic, finely chopped

Vegetable oil for frying

Yoghurt Sauce:

1 bunch chives, finely chopped

200g plain yoghurt

3 tbs fresh mint, chopped

3 tsp grated ginger

1 clove of garlic

Method:

To make falafe mixture:

Soak beans and chickpeas in one litre cold water for 24 hours. Drain and rinse well.

In a food processor, process the broad beans and chickpeas with a half teaspoon sea salt until they are the consistency of coarse, sticky breadcrumbs. Add coriander, spices, ginger, chilli, onion and garlic and process until a bright green paste with a fine crumb; the paste should not be smooth. Place in the refrigerator for half an hour before frying.

Half fill a saucepan with oil over a high heat and heat to 180°C. Shape falafe mixture into small patties and fry seven to eight minutes until a deep crunchy brown. Remove and drain well on a paper towel.

For the Sauce:

Combine all ingredients and store in the refrigerator until required.

Seared Beef & Pickled Ginger Leafy Salad

This dish makes a lovely light summer lunch or is ideal for parties as a starter served in Asian spoons.

Ingredients:

1/4 cup soy sauce

2 cloves garlic, minced

3 tbs rice wine vinegar

4 tbs freshly-squeezed orange juice (about 1 orange)

500g fillet or rump or porterhouse, trimmed of fat (approx 2cm thick)

Sea salt and pepper

1 tbs vegetable oil

2 oranges, segmented and all pith removed

1/2 cup pickled ginger slices

1 bunch of baby small-leafed rocket or baby cress, trimmed and rinsed

Method:

In a shallow dish combine soy sauce, garlic, two tablespoons vinegar and two tablespoons orange juice. Add the beef and turn to coat, then season with salt and pepper. Cover with plastic wrap and marinate for at least two hours or overnight.

Coat a skillet with vegetable oil and place over a high heat. When skillet is hot, remove the beef from the marinade and wipe away excess marinade. Add the beef to the hot skillet and sear for three to four minutes without moving per side for medium rare. Transfer to a cutting board and let rest for five minutes. Slice beef against the grain into 1/2cm thickness. Combine remaining orange juice and rice wine vinegar for vinaigrette. Toss orange segments, pickled ginger, rocket and beef with the vinaigrette.

the curcuma

Common Varieties:

Curcuma alismatifolia – Siam Tulip; *Curcuma cordata* – Jewel of Thailand; *Curcuma longa (or domestica)* – Turmeric; *Curcuma rubescens* – Ruby Ginger; *Curcuma sumatrana* – Olena Ginger.

There are around 80 species of curcuma, a genus of the *Zingiberaceae* family. Curcumas, although possessing exquisite flowers, are largely grown for their showy foliage owing to the actual flowers growing close to the ground and being quite hidden. This is of course with exception to the most common curcuma, turmeric, the vivid orange rhizome that is the source of the edible spice that is also used as a colourant. Curcumas are a deciduous tropical plant that has a predisposition as shady undergrowth. What is commonly referred to as the flower is in fact a stunning bract from which the somewhat smaller and daintier flowers emerge.

Steamed Scallops with Ginger & Garlic

Scallops make an impressive starter to any meal. Serve with slices of fresh, crusty bread to soak up the left-over juices.

Ingredients:

2 tbs peanut oil

3 cloves garlic, chopped

6 scallops on the shell, cleaned

1 small red chilli, sliced

6 slices pickled ginger

Sauce:

45ml soy sauce

1 tsp sugar

1 small red chilli, finely chopped

Garnish:

2 tbs spring onions, finely sliced

6 coriander leaves.

Method:

In a small frying pan, heat the oil, add the garlic and fry until golden. Pour a spoonful of garlic and oil over each scallop, add a little sliced chilli and top with pickled ginger slices. Cover and steam in steamer over simmering water for three to five minutes or until the scallops are just firm.

While the scallops steam, mix together the soy sauce, sugar and chilli.

When scallops are cooked, remove carefully from the steamer and place on a dish and drizzle with the sauce, then garnish with spring onions and coriander leaves.

Serve with fresh, crusty bread.

Tuna Tartare

For this recipe it is important to buy the absolute freshest in sashimi-grade tuna as it will be eaten raw. These yummy morsels make excellent hors d'oeuvres, the pickled ginger complimenting the tuna well.

Ingredients:

1 sheet shortcrust pastry

1 tbs black sesame seeds

150g fillet of sashimi-grade tuna, diced into 1/2cm dice

1 tsp fish sauce

2 tbs chives, finely chopped

1 tbs dill, finely chopped

1 tbs pickled ginger, finely sliced

2 tbs salmon roe

Method:

Sprinkle shortcrust pastry sheet with sesame seeds and use the light pressure of a rolling pin to push them into the pastry. Cut shortcrust pastry sheet into 5cm x 5cm squares. Pinch corners of pastry together and bake in an oven at 180°C for approximately 10 minutes or until golden in colour. Allow to cool. Combine tuna, fish sauce, chives, dill and pickled ginger in a bowl. To serve spoon a ball of tuna mix onto baked shortcrust pastry cases and garnish with salmon roe.

Tempura Oysters

This tempura mix strays a little from the traditional but is quick and easy. Make sure the oil isn't too hot as rice flour will burn easily. The tempura mix will be enough to make in excess of 12 oysters.

Ingredients:

¼ cup rice flour

¾ cups self-raising flour

1 tbs Buderim Ginger Refresher

1 cup sparkling mineral water, cold

12 oysters

Oil for deep-frying

Method:

Sift the rice flour and self-raising flour into a bowl. Add the Ginger Refresher to the mineral water. Make a well in the centre and slowly pour in ginger mix stirring the flour in from the sides. When well combined, chill in the refrigerator for an hour. The oysters should be fried directly prior to serving. When ready, heat the oil. When the oil is hot, dip each oyster into the batter and then straight into the oil, turning over when golden. Do small batches at a time. When each oyster is golden, remove from the oil and drain on absorbent paper and serve immediately. Serve with a soy dipping sauce or lemon juice. See notes on Buderim Ginger Refresher on page 47.

the heliconia

Common Varieties:

Heliconia angusta – Yellow Christmas or Red Holiday; *Heliconia psittacorum cv.* – varieties such as Andromeda, Blush, Sassy and Petra; *Heliconia rostrata* – Hanging Lobster Claws; *Heliconia stricta* – Lobster Claw Heliconias.

Heliconias include a wide spectrum of exotic tropical flowers of which the banana leaf-like foliage can reach up to six metres in height. Their family, the *Heliconaceae* has more than 300 varieties amongst their 89 recognised species.

The elegant flowerheads are waxy boat-like bracts that stand erect or hang pendant-like. The actual flower is quite inconspicuous being a rather ordinary curved tube in comparison to its often breathtakingly vibrant bracts. Heliconias grow and flower prolifically in tropical climates with the aid of organic matter and moderate watering.

Moroccan Chick Pea Soup

This is a definite favourite for me. The ginger really lifts the flavours in this soup. It can be served by itself as a hearty meal with fresh, crusty bread or as a starter.

Ingredients:

1 tbs olive oil

1 brown onion, finely chopped

2 garlic cloves, crushed

1 tbs grated ginger

1 1/2 tsp ground cumin

1 1/2 tsp ground coriander

1 tsp ground turmeric

1/2 tsp sweet paprika

1/4 tsp ground cinnamon

1/4 cup plain flour

4 cups water

3 cups vegetable stock

600g canned chickpeas, rinsed and drained

800g canned whole peeled tomatoes, undrained and crushed

1 tbs grated lemon rind

2 tbs lemon juice

1 tbs chopped coriander leaves

Fresh bread to serve

Chives, to garnish

Method:

Heat oil in a large saucepan and cook onion, garlic and ginger on medium heat, stirring until onion softens. Add spices and cook, stirring until fragrant.

Add flour, stirring constantly until mixture bubbles. Gradually stir in water and stock. Cook, stirring until mixture boils and thickens. Reduce heat and simmer, uncovered for five minutes.

Add chickpeas and undrained tomatoes and return mixture to the boil. Reduce heat and simmer, uncovered, for 10 minutes or until soup thickens. Add lemon rind and juice. Just before serving, stir through the coriander. When ladled into bowls, drizzle with a little extra virgin olive oil.

Chicken & Corn Soup with Ginger & Basil

A bowl of soup is one of the most relaxing and comforting dishes you can serve. This soup is almost a chowder and if served with crusty bread, would make a sensational meal.

Ingredients:

200g cooked chicken

1 litre chicken stock

2 tbs grated ginger

2 tbs cornflour

280g can creamed sweet corn

1 cup thinly sliced spring onion

2/3 cup packed basil leaves, chopped

Salt & pepper to taste

Garnish: basil leaves and extra grated ginger

Method:

Slice the chicken finely. Bring the stock to the boil and add grated ginger. Mix the cornflour to a smooth paste with three tablespoons of cold water and stir this into the stock until it boils and thickens.

Add the corn, spring onions, and basil. Season with salt and pepper to taste. Add the chicken meat and heat through. Serve in deep bowls topped with a sprig of basil and a sprinkle of grated ginger.

the  etlingera

Common Varieties:

Etlingera elatior – Red or Pink Torch Ginger or Walking Stick Ginger, other *elatior* species include Thai Queen, Yamamoto and Siam Rose.

The *Etlingera* is arguably the most majestic of the gingers, incorporating about 70 species within the *Zingiberaceae* family, the most common of which is the Torch Ginger. Magnificent tall stems emerge directly from the rhizomes in amongst huge leafy stems that reach enormous heights. Its huge crown shaped, usually a striking red or a beautiful soft pink, inflorescence is almost like an immense waxy rose. Its fleshy bracts peeling open slightly to reveal tiny intricate flowers.

Torch Ginger flowers are also edible and are often used in Asian cuisine.

Summer Prawns

These prawns can be cooked on the barbecue or stir-fried or as a novelty placed on skewers. They make an excellent light summer lunch.

Ingredients:

500g green prawns

3 spring onions

1 tbs Buderim Ginger Refresher

1/2 a lime, grated rind and juice

1/4 cup coriander leaves, shredded

Fresh chilli, to taste, sliced

Sea salt and freshly ground black pepper

Macadamia oil

Method:

Peel and de-vein prawns leaving tail. Slice spring onions diagonally. Combine other ingredients for the marinade and pour over prawns. Refrigerate for 30 minutes to one hour. Stir-fry in a little oil, grill or barbecue until opaque. Serve with steamed rice, salad or stir-fried vegetables.

Notes:

Buderim Ginger Refresher is a Ginger syrup produced by Buderim Ginger. It can be substituted with any ginger cordial. Ginger beer can also be used although it is not as concentrated.

Ginger & Coconut Rice

Ingredients:

2 cups long grain rice

2 1/2 cups water

1 tbs Buderim Ginger Crushed Ginger in Lemon Juice

3 tbs powdered coconut milk

Method:

Place all ingredients into a rice cooker and cook according to instructions for your machine. Or, place in a bowl in the microwave for 10 minutes on high.

Rest and stir.

Notes:

Buderim Ginger Crushed Ginger in Lemon Juice can be substituted with 1tbs freshly grated ginger and 1/2 tbs lemon juice.

Glass Noodle Salad with Barbecue Prawns

In my opinion seafood and ginger were born to be together and even more so when combined with other fresh, zesty flavours. This recipe boasts quite a number of ingredients but is surprisingly easy to make.

Ingredients:

For the Prawns:

250g green tiger prawns, peeled with tails intact

1 tbs fish sauce

1 clove garlic, crushed

2 tbs Buderim Ginger Mango & Ginger Conserve

1 tbs lime juice

1 tbs pineapple oil (optional)

Glass Noodle Salad:

6 dried shitake mushrooms

2 tbs ginger, grated

1 star anise

2 spring onions, finely sliced

1/2 tsp sesame oil

1 tbs rice vinegar

1 tsp sugar

Method:

For the Prawns:

Combine all ingredients and marinate for one hour. Barbecue prawns on a hot grill for approximately two minutes each side.

For the Glass Noodle Salad:

Cover dried mushrooms in water for 20 minutes, remove woody stems. Place mushrooms and liquid in a saucepan with grated ginger, star anise, spring onions and sesame oil and simmer for 20 minutes, until mushrooms are luscious. Then thinly slice the mushrooms and set aside.

Mix rice vinegar and sugar and marinate the sliced onion. Set aside. Combine lime juice, palm sugar, crushed ginger in lemon juice, garlic, fish sauce and lime kaffir leaves and set aside.

Pour boiling water over bean thread noodles and allow to soak for six minutes. Strain and set aside.

Place the prawns, sliced mushrooms and bean thread noodles in a bowl with the remaining ingredients. Toss well to combine thoroughly. Serve.

continued p.51...

1 purple onion, thinly sliced

3 tbs lime juice

2 tbs palm sugar

2 tsp Buderim Ginger Crushed Ginger in Lemon Juice

3 cloves garlic, crushed

3 tbs fish sauce

4 kaffir lime leaves, shredded

250g pkt bean thread noodles

1 carrot, finely julienned

1 cucumber, peeled and seeded and finely julienned

1 red capsicum, finely julienned

1 cup sunflower sprouts

1/2 cup roasted peanuts

1 cup coriander leaves

1 cup mint leaves

Notes:

Bean thread noodles are also known as glass noodles or vermicelli noodles (not rice vermicelli) or mung bean noodles. These noodles are made from mung bean starch and tapioca starch and has no wheat product.

If you have difficulty obtaining a Buderim Ginger Mango & Ginger Conserve, an easy substitute is to create you own by blending a ginger conserve with a mango conserve, although a ginger conserve by itself is equally pleasing. Buderim Ginger Crushed Ginger in Lemon Juice can be substituted with two teaspoons freshly grated ginger and one teaspoon lemon juice.

Fish Baked in Corn Husks

I love preparing fish in this method as the corn husks really help retain the moisture of the fish, as well as infusing the flesh with its own subtle flavour. Although prising the corn out of its husk without damaging it is a little fiddly, preparation can be done well in advance.

Ingredients:

4 corn cobs, in their husks

500g snapper fillets

1 tbs ginger, grated

1 clove garlic, finely sliced

2 tsp fish sauce

1 chilli, finely chopped

1 tbs lemongrass, finely sliced

4 lemon slices

4 tsp butter

2 tbs coriander, chopped

Salt & pepper

Extra lemon grass stalk for tying or raffia

Method:

Gently extract the cob from the husks without damaging the actual husk. This can be done by slicing an opening down the husk and prising the cob away from the stem with a sharp knife. It is important to not pierce or damage the husk, otherwise it will not retain the juices.

Preheat oven to 200°C. Cut fish fillets into medium-sized chunks and place evenly into the cavity of each of the four husks. Sprinkle each fish with a quarter of each of the ingredients, placing the lemon slices on the very top. Pull sides of the husk together and tie ends with the lemongrass stalks or raffia. Place filled husks on a greased baking tray and bake at 200°C for 15-20 minutes.

Serve with hot corn cobs basted with butter.

the costus

Common Varieties:

Costus barbatus – Spiral Ginger; *Costus comosus* – Red Tower Ginger; *Costus speciosus* – Crepe Ginger; *Costus spicatus* – Indianhead Ginger; *Costus stenophylus* – Red Snake Ginger.

The *costus* is part of the *Costaceae* family of which there are over 70 species. A lush evergreen plant, it produces attractive spiralling leafy stems that have a soft velvet under-leaf. The *Costus'* maze of beautiful flowers can vary quite dramatically, from soft crepe-like frills to spectacular trumpets of every shape and colour. The flowers emerge from a pinecone-like inflorescence that usually appears at the top of the stem, though some do shoot directly from the rhizome itself. They generally prefer a sheltered position in the garden, but will grow quite well in a sunny position providing they receive adequate watering.

Moroccan Style Roast Racks of Lamb

There are some great earthy flavours with this dish. The turmeric and ginger complement each other well. If you can get a hold of fresh turmeric use it as an alternative to the dry, as it has a much superior flavour. A good butcher will prepare the racks of lamb to your specifications.

Ingredients:

6 racks of lamb (4 cutlets each)

Marinade:

30g coriander leaves

3 cloves garlic, crushed

1 tbs grated ginger

1 tsp ground black pepper

1/2 tsp each of cumin, paprika and turmeric

Good pinch of saffron threads

6 tbs virgin olive oil

2 tbs lemon juice

Method:

Preheat oven to 200°C. Trim the lamb racks of all fat and sinew. Scrape the bones clean. Mix the marinade ingredients into a small bowl, then pat onto the lamb racks firmly. Leave to marinate in a snug-fitting container, covered overnight or for at least three to four hours in the refrigerator.

Lift the racks from the marinade container and place in roasting pan in a hot oven for 15-20 min or longer if preferred well done. Remove from oven, loosely cover with foil and rest for five minutes.

Serve with carrots cooked in a little chicken stock with pre-cooked chickpeas dizzled with olive oil.

Garnish with broad leaf parsley.

Char Grilled Chicken Breast with Ginger Glaze and Thai Coconut & Ginger Sauce

The sauce in this recipe is exquisite and tastes great with seafood as well. It also freezes well so it can be saved for later, if you have any left over.

Ingredients:

1 tbs Buderim Ginger Ginger, Lemon & Lime Marmalade

1 tbs soy sauce

1 tbs lime juice

4 chicken breasts, trimmed

For the sauce:

1 onion, finely chopped

1 clove garlic, finely chopped

2 tbs grated ginger

1 bunch coriander, thoroughly washed

2 lime kaffir leaves, shredded finely

2 red chillis, de-seeded and finely chopped

1 tbs peanut oil

450ml coconut milk

1/2 tsp turmeric powder

1 tbs lime juice

3 tsp fish sauce

Method:

Combine marmalade, soy and lime juice and marinate the chicken breasts in it for at least one hour. Char grill the chicken on a barbecue or on a hot plate for 10-15 minutes basting with the marinade.

For the Sauce:

In a food processor add onion, garlic and ginger and process before adding stem and roots of coriander, lime leaves and chilli and continue to process. Heat oil in a pan and add processed ingredients and gently fry for five minutes.

Add coconut milk, turmeric, lime juice and fish sauce and reduce to a simmer for a further five minutes or continue to cook and reduce to desired thickness. Add chopped coriander leaves.

Makes two cups of sauce.

Notes:

If you are finding it difficult to obtain a Buderim Ginger Ginger, Lemon and Lime Marmalade, your own combination can be created by combining a plain ginger marmalade with a lemon/lime marmalade.

the  alpinia

Common Varieties:

Alpinia caerulea – Australian Native Ginger; *Alpinia galaga* – Greater Galangal; *Alpinia nutans* – Dwarf Cardamom; *Alpinia purpurata* – Red Ginger or Ostrich Plume Ginger; *Alpinia zerumbert* – Shell Ginger.

The *Alpinia* boasts more than 230 species to its genus, making it the largest in the *Zingiberaceae* family. They are grown from large rhizomes forming medium-to-large plants that thrive in sheltered or semi-shaded positions.

The orchid-like flowers usually emerge from the previous year's growth and form spectacular clusters of waxy buds that one by one open into extraordinarily detailed flowers. The flowers are not as fragrant as other gingers but the aromatic foliage for which it is known makes up for it.

Mango & Ginger Chicken Wings with Cranberry & Ginger Couscous

The chicken wings by themselves make perfect finger food for parties or picnics. As for the couscous, it couldn't be easier to make and lends itself well as a light luncheon dish.

Ingredients:

1kg chicken wings

1 stalk of lemon grass, trimmed and thinly sliced

3 spring onions, thinly sliced

1 tbs peanut oil

1tsp sambal oelek or any chilli paste (optional)

2 tbs Buderim Ginger Mango and Ginger Conserve

2 tsp fish sauce

1 clove garlic, crushed

Salt and pepper to taste

Couscous:

1 1/2 cups couscous

1 1/2 cups boiling water

Method:

Cut wings into three pieces at joints; discard tips. Combine lemongrass, spring onions, oil, conserve, chilli or chilli paste (optional), fish sauce and garlic in a large bowl. Season with salt and pepper. Add chicken and toss to coat well. Cover and refrigerate for a minimum of 30 minutes.

Transfer chicken to a large, oiled baking tray. Cook uncovered in a hot oven (220°C) for about 35 minutes, turning frequently until chicken is browned all over and cooked through.

Place couscous in a heatproof bowl and add boiling water. Stand for five minutes until all the liquid is absorbed. Use a fork to fluff and separate couscous grains until fluffy.

Combine onions, parsley, coriander, almond slivers, craisins and ginger and add to couscous. Season with salt and pepper.

Dressing: (turn to next page for ingredients)
Combine garlic, lemon juice, olive oil and ginger marmalade in a screw top jar and shake well. Add dressing to salad and toss gently to combine.

cont'd p.67...

2 medium onions finely diced

1/2 cup coarsely chopped parsley

1/2 cup coarsely chopped coriander

75g toasted almond slivers

2 tbs craisins, roughly chopped

1 tbs glacé ginger, finely chopped

Dressing:

1 clove garlic

3 tbs lemon juice

2 tbs olive oil

1 heaped tbs Buderim Ginger Ginger Marmalade (softened in the microwave for 30 seconds)

Serve chicken wings on a dome of couscous. Chicken wings can be served warm or cold.

Serves 4 - 6

Notes:

If the Buderim Ginger Mango and Ginger Conserve is difficult to find, it can be substituted with a combination of a plain ginger and plain mango conserve. A ginger conserve can be used alone, although the mango provides just a little added depth of flavour.

Honeyed Ginger Pork with Broccoli & Cashews

Ingredients:

500g diced pork

1/2 cup cashews

250g broccoli, cut into
bite-sized flowerets

2 tbs peanut oil

Fresh mint

Marinade:

2 tbs honey

1 tbs soy sauce

1 tbs oyster sauce

1 tbs Buderim Ginger
Ginger Lemon & Lime
Marmalade

1 tsp Chinese five
spice powder

1 tbs Buderim Ginger
Crushed Ginger in
Lemon Juice

1 tbs Chinese rice wine
or dry sherry

1 clove crushed garlic

Sauce:

1/2 tbs cornflour

1 tbs soy sauce

1/4 cup water

1 chicken stock cube

Method:

Mix marinade ingredients together and marinate pork for at least one hour.

Heat oil in wok and stir-fry pork for approximately three minutes. Add broccoli and continue cooking on a high heat for a further three minutes. Add combined sauce ingredients to wok. Stir in cashews. Sprinkle with shredded mint.

Serve with Ginger & Coconut Rice (see page 47).

Notes:

If you are finding it difficult to obtain a Buderim Ginger Ginger, Lemon and Lime Marmalade, your own combination can be created by combining a plain ginger marmalade with a lemon or lime marmalade. Buderim Ginger Crushed Ginger in Lemon Juice can be substituted with one tablespoon of freshly grated ginger and half a tablespoon lemon juice.

the hedychium

Common Varieties:

Hedychium coronarium – White Butterfly Ginger or Ginger Lily; *Hedychium flavescens* – Yellow Ginger Lily; *Hedychium gardnerianum* – Kahili Ginger; *Hedychium cv.* – Luna Moth.

The *Hedychium* genus is comprised of more than 50 species in the family of *Zingiberaceaes*, The conical inflorescences appear at the end of lush banana leaf-like foliage each flowerhead displaying dozens of butterfly-shaped flowers that have a delightful and quite intense sweet fragrance. The individual flowers are often too fragile to make them viable cut flowers so they are usually grown as specimen plants or for their beautiful essential oils.

Best grown in partial shade, the rhizomes can be quite vigorous resulting in them being considered a pest in some areas.

Mini Pavlovas with Strawberries & Ginger

Such a decadent dessert - your own private mini pavlova, they are not hard to make and are definitely a show stopper! Any number of fruits can be used; mangoes, passionfruit or mixed berries they all complement ginger and vice versa.

Ingredients:

1 tbs cornflour

6 egg whites

1 pinch cream of tartar

350g caster sugar

1 tsp malt vinegar

1 tsp vanilla essence

1 punnet strawberries

1 tbs caster sugar extra

1 tbs glacé ginger, finely diced

½ tsp fresh ginger, finely grated

½ cup cream, whipped

Persian fairy floss or sifted icing sugar, to garnish

Method:

Line two baking trays with aluminium foil. Coat the foil with butter and sprinkle with cornflour, set aside. Preheat oven to 125°C. Beat egg whites with cream of tartar until stiff, taking care not to over beat. Slowly add caster sugar, small quantities at a time, beating as you go. When the mixture is extremely stiff and all the sugar has been added, add the vinegar and the vanilla essence and combine. Fold the sifted cornflour lightly into the mix.

Divide the mixture into eight mounds, four on each baking tray. Stack the mound high by dragging up the sides with the back of a spoon and scoop a hollow out of the centre. Place the trays into the oven and bake for approximately two to two-and-a-half hours at 125°C. The meringues should be hard when tapped. Allow to cool slowly in the switched-off oven with the door slightly ajar.

Slice four of the strawberries into ½cm slices. Place on a small dish and sprinkle with half of the extra caster sugar and glacé ginger. Set aside. Process the remaining strawberries in a blender with the last of the extra caster sugar and grated ginger until puréed. Set aside also. To serve, place each meringue on a dish. Fill the hollow of each meringue with a spoonful of whipped cream. Perch two or three of the sliced strawberries into the cream and scatter the remaining slices around the meringue. Sprinkle with any leftover glacé ginger. Drizzle the strawberry purée on top of the meringue and around the dish. Garnish with a tuft of Persian fairy floss or sifted icing sugar.

Eggnog & Glacé Ginger Ice-Cream

This is a great dessert on a hot summer day or as a cool alternative on Christmas Day replacing the more traditional Christmas pudding

Ingredients:

500ml milk

500ml cream

2 tsp vanilla extract

200g caster sugar

7 large egg yolks

1 tsp freshly ground nutmeg

2 tbs brandy

2 tbs rum

1 cup glacé ginger cut into small diced pieces

2 tbs toasted almond slivers

Method:

Heat milk, cream and vanilla, do not boil. In a double boiler combine sugar and egg yolks and whisk until combined and creamy. Add the heated milk and cream in a steady stream while continuing to whisk.

Cook custard, stirring constantly until the custard is thick enough to coat the back of a spoon. Allow the custard to cool and stir in the nutmeg, brandy, rum, glacé ginger and almonds. Chill.

When cold, churn in an ice-cream machine according to the manufacturer's instructions.

the foliage

Quite often the foliage of ginger plants can be almost as attractive as their flowers. Heliconias in particular have impressive banana-like leaves that are often quite colourfully striped or have contrasting veins and underleaf extending through to the stems. The curcumas' foliage is more obvious than its flower, the flowers being nestled in underneath, but its deep red veins and perfect spear-shaped leaves in some varieties make it a popular foliage plant.

The costus tends to have the most striking stems and they either spiral beautifully with soft downy leaves that are luxurious to touch or have bamboo-like striped and patterned stems that are vibrantly trimmed.

By far the most aromatic foliage, is that of the *Alpinia*, the Dwarf Cardamom in particular. In the garden one needs to just brush against it for the leaves to release the most delectable fragrance that lingeringly permeates the air.

Strawberry, Ginger & Coconut Tart

This is a very traditional recipe. It is great served hot with ice-cream though is equally as nice cold. Try serving it with some poached fruit.

Ingredients:

Dough:

125g butter

1/4 cup sugar

1 egg

1 1/2 cups self-raising flour

1 cup Buderim Ginger Mango & Ginger Conserve

Coconut Topping:

1 egg

1 cup sugar

1 cup desiccated coconut

Method:

Cream butter and sugar, add egg and beat well. Stir in the sifted flour and combine to form a soft dough. With lightly floured fingers press the dough into a greased 26cm tart tin extending the dough up the walls of the tin. Spread the Buderim Ginger Mango and Ginger Conserve over the dough.

In a bowl, beat the egg with the sugar until light in colour, fold in the coconut. Spoon the topping evenly over the jam and gently spread with a knife. Bake in a moderate oven 180°C degrees for 30-35 minutes. Leave in the tin until cold.

Serve the tart warm or cold with ice-cream or cream. This recipe can also be baked as a slice and cut and served in fingers.

Notes:

If the Buderim Ginger Mango and Ginger Conserve is difficult to obtain make a blend of your own by combining a plain ginger conserve with another fruit or berry conserve.

Ginger & Lime Friands

As a special treat serve the friands with their tops lifted and filled with a little ginger conserve and whipped cream. Sprinkle with icing sugar.

Ingredients:

*5 egg whites, beaten
until soft peaks*

1 cup almond meal

1/2 cup plain flour

1 tbs lime juice

180g butter, melted

250g icing sugar

Grated rind of 1 lime

*1/2 cup glacé ginger
roughly chopped*

2 tbs slivered almonds

Method:

Preheat oven to 190°C. Grease a friand tin. Mix all ingredients together except slivered almonds and fill each friand tin two thirds with the mixture. Sprinkle with the slivered almonds. Bake for 25 minutes or until golden and the friand has pulled away from the edges slightly.

Leave in the tin to cool.

Ginger Liqueur Truffles

Ingredients:

100g unsalted butter, chopped

125ml cream

300g dark chocolate, chopped

2 egg yolks

1 tbs Grand Marnier

1 tbs glacé ginger, finely diced

Cocoa powder

Method:

Combine butter and cream in a saucepan and heat gently until butter is melted and cream is bubbling. Remove from heat and add the chocolate. Cover pan and allow to stand until the chocolate is melted. Add the beaten egg yolks and return to stove on low heat, stirring until the mixture is thick and glossy. Remove from heat, stir in liqueur and ginger and allow to cool.

When the mixture is cool, refrigerate until solid enough to roll into small balls. Roll into small balls and then roll in cocoa powder until mixture is used.

Ginger & Apricot Rum Balls

Ingredients:

1/3 cup minced dried apricots

¼ cup dark rum

1 cup wafer crumbs

1 cup gingernut crumbs

¼ cup glacé ginger, finely diced

½ cup pecans, finely chopped

¼ cup light corn syrup

2 tbs dark rum, extra

¼ tsp ground ginger

1 cup finely chopped pecans, extra, lightly toasted

Method:

In a small covered saucepan bring the apricots and dark rum to the boil over medium heat and simmer for five minutes or until the rum is absorbed. In a large bowl combine the wafer crumbs, gingernut crumbs, glacé ginger, pecans, apricots, corn syrup, extra rum and ground ginger. Blend the mixture until it forms a firm ball. Shape rounded teaspoons of the mixture into balls, then roll balls in the extra pecans. Arrange the balls on a baking tray lined with baking paper and chill covered for two hours.

Store in an airtight container. The flavour improves if chilled for at least one day before serving.

Steamy Nights

There is nothing like a refreshing ginger cocktail on a hot summers day.

Ingredients:

20ml Buderim Ginger Refresher

30ml tequila

80ml orange juice

40ml water

15ml Galliano

Method:

Combine over ice in a tall glass.

Sangria

Ingredients:

5-6 oranges

1 lemon

1/4 cup sugar

1/4 cup Buderim Ginger Refresher

750ml shiraz or cabernet sauvignon

1/4 cup Cointreau or Grand Marnier

Method:

Using a potato peeler or zester remove rind from two oranges and the lemon. Place in a jug with sugar and bruise the rind with the back of a spoon. This leaches out the orange and lemon oil. Juice enough oranges to give 500ml of juice and add it to the jug with all remaining ingredients. Remove the peel after 30 minutes. Cut another orange into fine slices and add to the sangria.

Serve in a glass filled with ice.

Crimson Zing

Ingredients:

Ice cubes

30ml Buderim Ginger Refresher

30ml vodka

90ml cranberry juice

1/4 lime, juice only

Soda water

Method:

Add Ginger Refresher, vodka, cranberry juice and lime to a tall glass with ice cubes. Dilute with soda as desired.

Notes:

Ginger Refresher is a ginger syrup produced by Buderim Ginger. It can be substituted with any ginger cordial. Ginger beer can also be used - just omit the soda water.

the beautiful others

Common Varieties:

Calathea burlemarxii – Blue Ice Ginger; *Calathea crotalifera* – Red or Yellow Rattleshaker; *Dichorisandra spp.* - Blue Ginger; *Globba winitii* – Miniature Gingers including species such as Thai Beauty and Princess Kim.

Blue Ginger and the wonderful range of *Calatheas* are not true gingers, though they are often referred to as gingers. Spectacular as they are, they are most definitely worthy of a place in any ginger garden.

Globbas, on the other hand, are true gingers. Commonly called miniature gingers, they are a genus comprising up to 100 species of small ginger plants amongst the family of *Zingiberaceae*. Although small, they produce a pretty cluster of tubular flowers that escape in masses from their pendulous colourful bracts.

Dichorisandra ssp. - 'Blue Ginger'

Alpinia nutans - Dwarf Cardamom

Alpinia zerumbert - Shell Ginger

Alpinia nutans - Dwarf Cardamom

Zingiber spectabile - 'Golden Beehive Ginger'

Zingiber ottensii - 'Cocoa Delight'

Zingiber spectabile

Zingiber ottensii - 'Cocoa Delight'

Costus chartaceous - 'Christmas Costus'

Costus barbatus - 'Red Tower Ginger'

Costus stenophylus - 'Red Snake Ginger'

Costus Curvibracteatus

Costus glaucous

Costus pictus

Costus species

Costus speciosus - 'Crepe Ginger'

Heliconia psittacorum -
Parrots Beak 'Petra'

Heliconia psittacorum -
Parrots Beak 'Sassy'

Heliconia angusta - Red Holiday

Heliconia angusta - Yellow Christmas

Heliconia species

Heliconia species

Heliconia latispatha

Heliconia rostrata - Hanging Lobster
Claw

Heliconia stricta

Heliconia stricta

Heliconia caribaea

Heliconia chartacea - Sexy Pink

Heliconia chartacea - Sexy Pink

Heliconia bourgaena

Calathea burle-marxii - Blue Ice

Etlingera elatior

Curcuma species

Curcuma alismatifolia - 'Tropical Snow'

Curcuma 'Chocolate Zebra'

Curcuma species

Curcuma species

Curcuma 'Pink Pearl'

Curcuma alismatifolia - Siam Tulip

Curcuma species

Curcuma cordata

Curcuma 'Voodoo Magic'

Curcuma 'Anita'

Curcuma roscoeana 'Pride of Burma'

Hedychium

Hedychium Gaardenianum - 'Kahili Ginger'

Globba winitii - 'Guardian Angel'

Globba winitii - Princess Kim